What a Load of Rubbish

Written by Claire Llewellyn

CW00840112

Contents

Looking at rubbish

This book is all about rubbish. We all have rubbish
and we put it in the bin. Sometimes we put
too much rubbish in the bin.

Every day we throw away
newspapers, boxes, bottles
and jars, food and old clothes.
Many of these things can be
made into new things.
This is called recycling.

This book tells you how
you can help to recycle
your rubbish. It tells
you what you can do!

Recycling old paper

Newspapers, magazines, some bags and boxes are all made from paper. Some of this waste paper can be taken to a paper bank to be recycled into new paper.

What to do:
1. Sort waste paper from the rest of your rubbish.
2. Save it in a bag or bin.
3. Once a week, take it to the paper bank.

The paper is taken away when the bank is full and made into recycled paper. Recycled paper can be used to make many things.

Some recycled paper can be used in schools.

Recycling old glass

Bottles and jars are made from glass.
Some people throw them away when they are empty.
This is a waste. Old glass can be taken to a bottle bank and recycled into new glass.

What to do:
1. Sort glass jars and bottles from the rest of your rubbish.
2. Save them in a bin.
3. Once a week, take them to the bottle bank.

At a bottle bank there is a green bin for green glass, a brown bin for brown glass and a white bin for clear glass. The glass is taken away when the bottle banks are full. It is melted and made into new glass.

Glass milk bottles are used over and over again.

Recycling old food

A lot of food is too good to put in the bin. Bits of fruit and vegetable will rot down and make compost for the garden. Compost helps plants to grow.

What to do:
1. Save all your old fruit and vegetable peelings in a bowl.
2. When it is full empty the bowl into a compost bin.
3. Every six months, take the compost out of the bin, and put it on the garden.

Compost is dug into the garden.

Recycling old clothes

Some people throw away their clothes when they no longer fit. This is a waste. Other people can use some of these clothes. If the clothes are too old they can be taken to a clothes bank to be recycled.

What to do:
1. Sort your old clothes into two piles: the good and the not-so-good.
2. Take the good clothes to a charity shop like Oxfam, where people can buy them.
3. Take the old clothes to a clothes bank.

The clothes in the clothes bank are taken away and sorted.
They can then be made into new kinds of cloth.

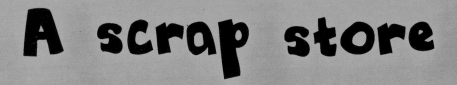

A scrap store

Another way to recycle is to use a scrap store. This is a place where people from shops or factories take things that they do not want. It may be boxes, cloth or buttons – anything that is too good to throw away.

People from children's clubs come to see what's there. They take away anything that they can use to make toys or arts and crafts.

This caterpillar was made from recycled card and paper cups.

Recycling chart

PLEASE
RECYCLE

Waste goods	Take to
Newspapers and other paper goods	Paper bank
Glasses and jars	Bottle bank
Bits of fruit and vegetable	Compost bin
Old clothes	Charity shop
Old clothes	Clothes bank

What happens to them?	Recycled goods
They are cut up and mixed with water to make recycled paper	Toilet rolls, tissues, envelopes
They are melted to make new glass	Bottles, jars
They rot down into compost	A good food for garden plants
People buy them to use again	–
They are broken down into little bits to make new cloth	New thread and cloth

Index